My First Activity Book

This book belongs to:

DK

LONDON, NEW YORK, MUNICH, MELBOURNE AND DELHI

Project Editor Lindsay Kent
Designer Lynne Moulding
Publishing Manager Simon Beecroft
Senior Art Editor Lisa Lanzarini
Category Publisher Alex Allan
Production Rochelle Talary
DTP Designer Lauren Egan

First published in Great Britain in 2006 by
Dorling Kindersley Limited,
80 Strand, London WC2R 0RL
A Penguin Company

06 07 08 09 10 11 9 8 7 6 5 4 3 2 1

A CIP catalogue record for this book is
available from the British Library.

ISBN-13: 978-1-40531-351-3
ISBN-10: 1-4053-1351-X

Reproduced by Media Development and Printing, Ltd., UK
Printed and bound in China by Hung Hing

Discover more at
www.dk.com

Contents

Before you begin

It's so much fun making things with your friends. On this page you'll find out what you need to get started. It's always a good idea to be well prepared, because once you get going, you won't want to stop!

I can't wait to get started!

✋ A helping hand

You should always have an adult with you when you are making the projects to help you with the more tricky bits. It is especially important for an adult to help you with the steps marked with a hand symbol.

Staying neat and tidy

Using paints, glue and glitter can get messy so before you start your project you should change into old clothes or wear an apron so you don't get dirty.

Oops! Paints spill if you're not careful.

Be careful

Remember to take care when you are using scissors to cut things out. Always use safety scissors that have rounded tips.

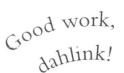

Good work, dahlink!

Making a mess!

Always check with an adult before you start a craft project as you might need to cover your work surface with newspaper or an old sheet so you don't make it messy.

Enjoy yourself!

Being creative is lots of fun, epecially if you're making things with your friends. Don't worry if your finished project doesn't look perfect – the most important thing is to enjoy yourself while you're making it.

They are lovely!

Beautiful beads

I love to wear pretty jewellery, especially beads I have made myself. I just know that you and your friends will have fun creating this delightful necklace!

You will need:

- ★ 1 cup of plain flour
- ★ 1 cup of salt
- ★ ½ cup of water
- ★ mini cookie cutters
- ★ cocktail stick
- ★ acrylic paints
- ★ paintbrushes
- ★ 50cm length of narrow ribbon
- ★ large embroidery needle

1. Turn the oven on to 110°C (225°F/Gas ¼).

2. Put the flour, salt and water into a bowl and stir together with a spoon until you have a firm dough.

Wiggle the stick!

3. Roll out the dough and use cookie cutters to cut out your beads. You can also use your hands to make beads in any shape you like!

4. Use a cocktail stick to make a hole through each bead. Wiggle the stick around in the hole to make it big enough for the ribbon to fit through.

5. Place the beads in the oven for two hours. When they are cooked, remove the beads from the oven and leave them until they have cooled down. Now you are ready to paint them!

You can paint pretty patterns on them!

The needle makes it easy to thread the beads onto the ribbon.

I love beads too!

6. Take your ribbon and tie a knot 10cm from one end. Thread the other end of the ribbon through the needle.

7. Thread about 20 beads onto the ribbon. Leave 10cm of ribbon after the last bead so you can tie the necklace around your neck.

Handy hankies

These hankies are so easy to make and are lovely and useful gifts for Mum, Dad, Grandpa and Grandma. Miss Lilly adores them too!

I've made this hanky for Grandma.

You will need:

★ scrap paper
★ plain white hanky
★ fabric ink pens
★ ribbons
★ safety scissors

1. Think of a drawing or pattern for your hanky and practice it on paper until you are happy with it. If you're making the hanky as a gift for someone, think of a design that they would like.

You can look through your favourite books to get some ideas.

2. Spread the hanky out on some scrap paper. Draw your design on it with the fabric pens.

3. When the ink is dry you can use colourful ribbons to make the hanky look extra special. Choose some ribbon that matches your design and tie it around the hanky with a pretty bow.

Grandpa always carries a hankie in his pocket.

Door decorations

These pink hearts are my tip top favourites. You can use them to decorate your bedroom door or give them as gifts to someone you really truly love!

You will need:

- ★ 2 sheets of A4 card
- ★ pencil
- ★ safety scissors
- ★ 3 50cm lengths of ribbon
- ★ PVA glue
- ★ spatula
- ★ 3D fabric paint or acrylic paint

1. On a sheet of card, draw one large heart shape and two small heart shapes. Cut each shape out.

2. Now take the second sheet of card and draw around each of the hearts. Cut these shapes out too so you have six heart shapes altogether – two large ones and four small ones.

3. Tie a bow in the centre of one of the pieces of ribbon. Repeat this with the other two pieces of ribbon.

4. Take a large heart and spread glue on one side of it. Place just the ends of a bow on the heart and stick the other large heart on top. Repeat this with the smaller heart shapes, so you have three heart shapes in total.

5. Decorate the hearts with a pretty pattern using the fabric paint. When you have finished, leave the paint to dry. Fabric paint looks pretty because it makes your pattern raised and 3D but you could use acrylic paint instead.

To stick the hearts to your bedroom door just put a little piece of double-sided tape on the centre of each bow.

Butterfly card

This sparkly card is lots of fun to make and as pretty as a real butterfly. You can use it as a birthday card, a thank you card or even party invitation!

I like to make cards for my friends!

You will need:

★ 2 sheets of white A4 paper
★ 3 sheets of A4 paper in different colours
★ pencil
★ safety scissors
★ PVA glue
★ sequins
★ envelope

1. To make a template, fold a sheet of white paper in half. On one side draw the outline of half a butterfly and cut it out. Repeat with the other piece of paper but this time make the butterfly shape a little smaller.

2. Open out the biggest template and draw around it on a sheet of coloured paper. On a sheet of different coloured paper, draw around the smaller template. Fold the shapes in half along the centre.

3. Glue the smaller butterfly shape onto the bigger one. Turn the card over so the smaller butterfly is underneath and fold the card in half.

4. Draw four large ovals and lots of little circles on the last sheet of coloured paper. Cut them out and glue them onto the wings to make a pretty pattern.

5. Now it time to make the wings look beautiful – just like a real butterfly. Use the glue to stick little sequins onto the oval and circle shapes and see how they sparkle!

6. When the glue has dried you can write in the card. It could be a birthday card, a party invitation, or a thank you card. Whatever you use it for, your friends and family will love it!

I'm making a party invitation!

I'm glad you like the card I made you!

Come to my birthday party!

Great gift wrap

It's great fun to give gifts, and it's even more fun if you make the wrapping paper yourself. Here are three ways to create your own handmade gift wrap.

What pretty gifts!

You will need:

★ 3 large sheets of paper
★ pencil
★ sheet of thin foam
★ empty matchbox
★ glitter
★ safety scissors
★ acrylic paints
★ PVA glue
★ paintbrushes
★ hole punch
★ A4 card
★ ribbons

Printing shapes

1. Draw a shape onto the foam sheet and cut it out. Glue the foam shape onto the matchbox and leave it to dry.

2. Pour a little paint onto an old plate and gently dip the matchbox into the paint until the foam shape is coated. Extra paint can be removed with a paintbrush.

3. Press the shape down firmly on the paper and repeat until the paper is covered. Leave the paper to dry.

Splatter patterns

1. This can be messy so it's a good idea to cover the work surface with newspaper and put on an apron.

Be careful not to splatter the walls!

2. Add a little water to some paint so it's a bit runny. Dip the paintbrush in the paint and splatter the paper with the paint. Leave the paper to dry.

Glitter flowers

1. On a sheet of paper use the glue to draws pretty flower shapes.

2. Sprinkle glitter all over the glue, making sure that the glitter has stuck to the flower shapes. Gently shake the paper to remove any excess glitter.

Let's add lots of glitter!

3. Fill in the gaps with small dots of glue and add glitter as before. Leave the paper to dry.

Now turn the page!

Gift tags

1. Draw a rectangle on a piece of card that is 10cm high and 5cm wide. Using the scissors, cut the rectangle out.

2. Next, fold the rectangle in half so you have a square shape. Use the hole punch to make a hole in the top corner on the same side as the fold.

3. Using the same steps as before, decorate the outside of the tag so it matches your wrapping paper.

4. Cut a piece of ribbon that is 10cm long. Thread it through the hole in the tag and tie the ends together.

Mouselings love gifts and parties!

Everyone
loves pretty
packages!

Gifts will look wonderful
when you wrap them in your
handmade wrapping paper.
As a finishing touch, add pretty
ribbons and your gorgeous gift tags!

They look so pretty, it's a shame
to unwrap them!

Brilliant bag

I take my pretty bag wherever I go. It's perfect for carrying my ballet things. With my special decorations and an "A" for Angelina on the front, I'll never lose it!

You will need:

- ★ lilac felt, 20cm x 50cm
- ★ fabric glue
- ★ 2 30cm lengths of ribbon
- ★ card, 10cm x 10cm
- ★ pencil
- ★ pink felt, 10cm x 10cm
- ★ felt tip pen
- ★ selection of materials to decorate the bag (such as ribbons, felt, glitter, fabric flowers or buttons)

1. Take the rectangle of felt and fold it in half. Press down firmly to make a crease. Unfold the felt and spread glue along the two side edges of one half only.

Soon you'll have your own special bag!

2. Now carefully fold the felt in half, as you did before, and stick the two sides together. Press down firmly and leave the glue to dry overnight.

Press down hard!

3. To add handles to your bag, position the felt so the open end is at the top. Take the first piece of ribbon and glue one end about 5cm in from the left side of the bag. Glue the other end about 5cm from the right side. Turn the bag over and repeat with the other piece of ribbon.

4. After the glue has dried, turn the bag inside out. This is so you don't see any untidy edges where you've glued the bag together.

Now turn the page!

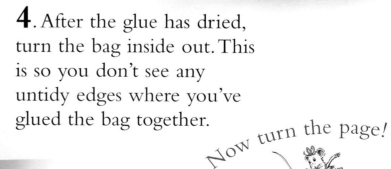

6. You can personalise your bag with the first letter of your name. First make a template by drawing the letter on a piece of card and cutting it out carefully.

7. Take the small piece of felt and draw around the template using a felt tip pen. Cut the letter out. Now turn the letter over, spread glue over the back of it and stick it to the front of your bag.

Look at all the pretty decorations!

Oooh – all my favourite colours!

8. You can decorate your bag using anything you like. Sewing shops sell lots of pretty things like little butterflies, fabric flowers, buttons, beads and ribbons, that will make your bag look brilliant. Decide on what you want to use and glue them on. Once you've finished decorating your bag, leave the glue to dry.

You can use
bags to store all
your special things,
like hair bands,
ballet slippers
and jewellery.

You can make bags in all sorts of
colours and sizes!

Cute hair clips

These cute hair clips are great fun to make, and you can add all sorts of glittery decorations. You'll really sparkle when you're wearing them!

You will need:

- ★ sheet of A4 paper
- ★ pencil
- ★ scissors
- ★ 3 sheets of felt (pink, purple and white)
- ★ felt tip pen
- ★ fabric glue
- ★ glitter
- ★ plain hair clip

1. On a piece of paper, draw a flower shape that's about 4cm high and 4cm wide. Draw a circle that fits on the centre of the flower and cut the shapes out.

2. Take the pink felt and use the pen to draw around the flower template. Do this again with the white felt. On the purple felt, draw around the circle template. Cut the shapes out.

I love sparkly hair clips!

3. Place the white flower on the pink one so you can see all eight petals, and glue them together. Glue the purple circle onto the centre of the white flower.

4. Add some sparkle by putting a spot of glue in the middle of the purple circle and sprinkle it with some glitter!

5. Put glue on the back of the flower and stick it to the end of a clip. Leave it to dry.

You can make special clips for your friends!

Fantastic flowers

I love flowers – they are beautiful, colourful and smell lovely too. You can make your very own fancy flower garland to brighten up your bedroom!

You will need:

* ★ safety scissors
* ★ pencil
* ★ PVA glue
* ★ A4 white card
* ★ 10 sheets of paper in various colours
* ★ 1m of wide ribbon

1. On the card draw two flower shapes, one slightly larger than the other. Now draw a circle for the centre of the flower and a leaf shape. Cut each shape out.

To make lots of shapes at once, fold the paper a few times before drawing round your template.

2. Draw around the templates on the sheets of coloured paper and cut the shapes out. Repeat until you have made ten of each shape.

3. Take a large flower and glue a smaller flower on top of it and then glue a circle onto the centre of it. Turn the flower over and stick a leaf shape to the back. Repeat until you have made ten flowers.

4. Glue the flowers to one side of the ribbon, leaving a gap of about 10cm between each one. Once the glue has completely dried, your flower garland is finished!

The flowers look so pretty wrapped around the bed!

Fun fairy outfit

Dressing up is the best fun ever, and every girl loves to be a pretty fairy. With a magical skirt, wand and a pair of twinkling wings you'll be a star!

Fairy skirt
You will need:

★ A4 paper
★ pencil
★ safety scissors
★ 1m netting
★ 2 pins
★ 60cm ribbon

★ PVA glue
★ small metalic stars or sequins to decorate

1. Draw a petal shape on the paper. Make the petal about 20cm long. Cut the shape out.

I can't wait to wear my fairy skirt!

2. Fold the netting a number of times so there are lots of layers. Attach the petal template to the netting using the pins and draw around it with the pencil. Cut the shapes out and repeat until you have 20 petals in total.

3. Glue two petals, one on top of the other, 20cm from the end of the ribbon. Glue two more petals to the ribbon so that they overlap the first ones a little. Repeat until you have about 20cm of ribbon left at the end.

The little stars make the skirt sparkle!

4. Now it's time to decorate your fairy skirt to make it look magical! Carefully glue a few little stars at the botom of each petal.

You can make your fairy outfit in any colour.

5. Once the glue has dried, you can put your skirt on. Just wrap it around your waist and tie a pretty bow in the ribbon.

Fairy wings

You will need:

★ diluted PVA glue (1 part glue to 3 parts water)
★ 10 sheets of tissue paper
★ clingfilm
  paintbrush
★ pencil
★ A4 paper

★ safety scissors
★ PVA glue
★ 5cm x 8cm cardboard

★ hole punch
★ two 40cm lengths of elastic
★ glitter and stars

1. Spread clingfilm on the table. Place two sheets of tissue paper on the clingfilm and use the paintbrush to cover them with the glue mixture. Repeat until all the tissue paper is stuck together.

2. Take the A4 paper and draw a large teardrop shape on it. Try to make the shape fill the whole page. Cut the shape out.

Fairies have delicate wings.

3. Once the tissue paper is dry, remove the clingfilm. Use the template to draw two tear drop shapes on the tissue paper. Cut both of the shapes out carefully.

4. Overlap the pointed ends of the two shapes and glue them together, to make wings.

5. Use the hole punch to make a hole in each corner of the cardboard. Thread a piece of elastic through the top and bottom holes on the left side and tie the ends together. Repeat this with holes on the right using the other piece of elastic.

6. Spread glue over the cardboard and stick in the centre of the wings. Make sure the knots on the elastic loops are hidden under the card when you stick it down. Leave the glue to dry.

I love wings too!

7. Turn the wings over and use the glitter and stars to decorate them. Make sure the glue has dried before you try your wings on.

Fairy wand

You will need:

- clingfilm
- sticky tape
- PVA glue
- diluted PVA glue
  (1 part glue to 3 parts water)
- 10 sheets of tissue paper
- paintbrush
- glitter

- A4 sheet white card
- pencil
- scissors
- 50cm ribbon
- small garden cane (or straw)

1. Spread clingfilm on the table. Place two sheets of tissue paper on the cling film and use the paintbrush to cover them with the glue mixture. Repeat until all the tissue paper is stuck together. While the paper is wet, sprinkle a little glitter over it. Leave it to dry.

2. Draw two star shapes on the card, one bigger than the other. Cut both shapes out.

3. Once the tissue paper is dry, remove it from the clingfilm. Place the large star on the tissue paper and draw around it and then cut it out.

Faries love to dance and play together!

4. Spread glue over the smaller card star and cover it with glitter. Once the glue is dry, stick the smaller star onto the larger one.

5. Cover the stick with glue and wrap the ribbon around it until it is covered. Use a piece of sticky tape to stick the star shape onto the stick.

Fairies wave their magic wands!

You and your friends can create your very own fairy dance!

Acknowledgements

Dorling Kindersley would like to thank the following
for their help in preparing this book:

The children and their parents who attended the photo shoot;
Dave King for his beautiful photographs and Sue Nicholson
for all her help with the craft projects.